Who Am I

Elizabeth Sprehe

WORDS MATTER
P U B L I S H I N G
OUR WORDS CHANGE THE WORLD

Words Matter Publishing
P.O. Box 531
Salem, Il 62881
www.wordsmatterpublishing.com

ISBN 13: 978-1-949809-24-4
ISBN 10: 1-949809-24-2

Library of Congress Catalog Card Number: 2019933732

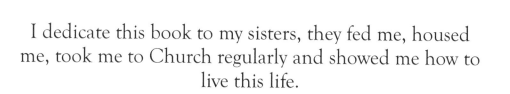

I dedicate this book to my sisters, they fed me, housed me, took me to Church regularly and showed me how to live this life.

Table of Contents

Who Am I

I haven't heard about you
Or a letter I've not received
I know that you are so busy
I hope that you aren't peeved.
I often think about you
And include you in my prayer
I ask the Lord to bless you
And keep you in his care.
So if you have some time
I'd love to hear from you
But if you don't, I understand
And I'm still your friend so true.

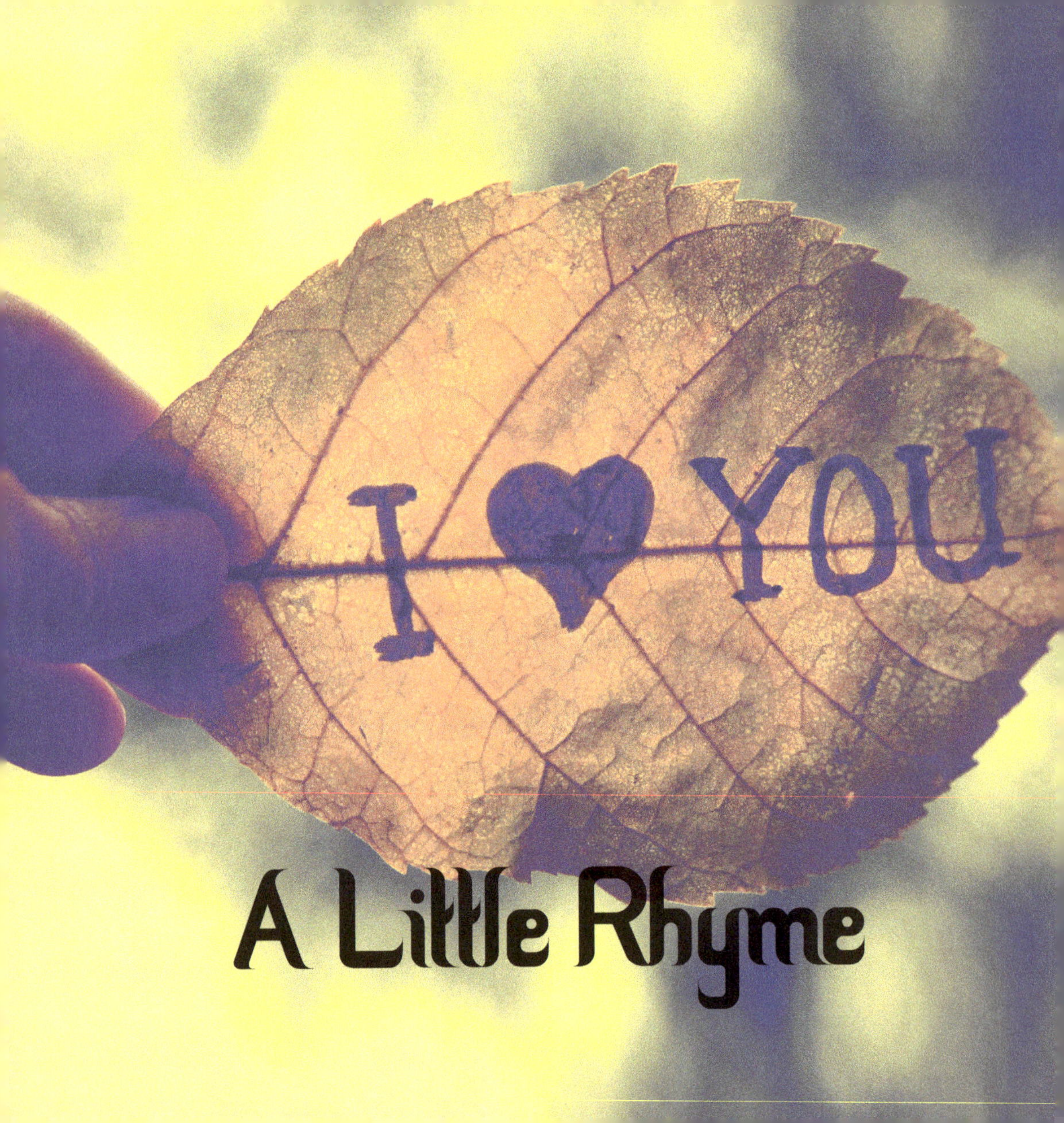

A Little Rhyme

Who Am I

Thought I'd just sit right here
Not waste my precious time
Not jumble up my brain
Or rhyme a little rhyme
Wouldn't tell those people near
How much I truly care
Or let them know of my love
They're in my every prayer
But then I thought again
Knew what I longed to do
I'd write this little rhyme
To say that I love you.

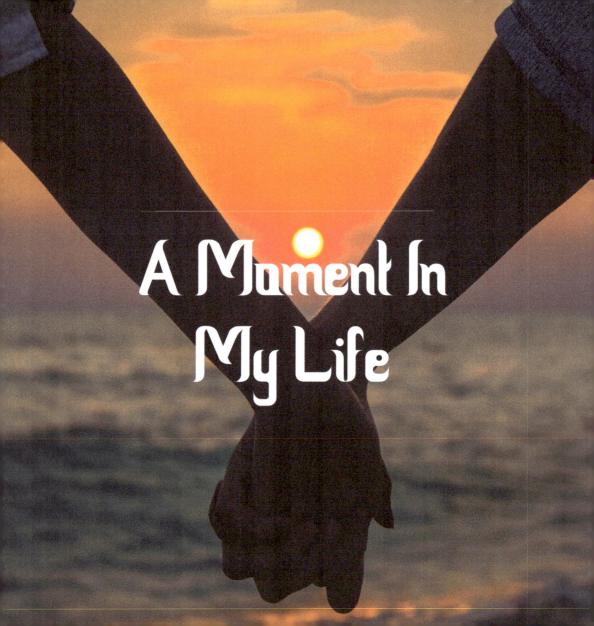

Just for a moment
You held me tenderly
For that lonely moment
We lived so happily
Just for a moment
We walked hand in hand
And for one moment
We lived a life so grand
Seems like for a moment
We'd found a love so true
And for that lovely moment
I loved you—only you.

A
Saint

Whenever I hear your loving voice near
It reminds me of my childhood years,
When I was young, in my mother's care
She'd give me love and always share,
She'd take the tie to hear my woe
Her prayers would follow wher'er I'd go,
When I'd return she was waiting for me
To kiss the hurt or patch the knee,
She'd read God's Word and pray each day
And guard each thing I'd do and say.
My mother was a saint, that's true
In fact, Lord, she was a lot like you.

A Sister

Some people touch our heart
We feel privileged to meet
They somehow nudge right in
And make our life complete
We know we can depend
On them for love and care
We feel new strength each day
From being in their prayers
So if I do not write
Or say kind words to you
I thank my God above
For a sister that is true.

A Young Mother's Lament

I go along full speed ahead without a care or worry
I charge right in and do all things, I'm always in a hurry
I must do this and get that done while it is still today
I need to do all that I can, after all, what will others say!
Somedays there's just no time to sit and dream and ponder
When will I get my turn, or will it come I wonder?

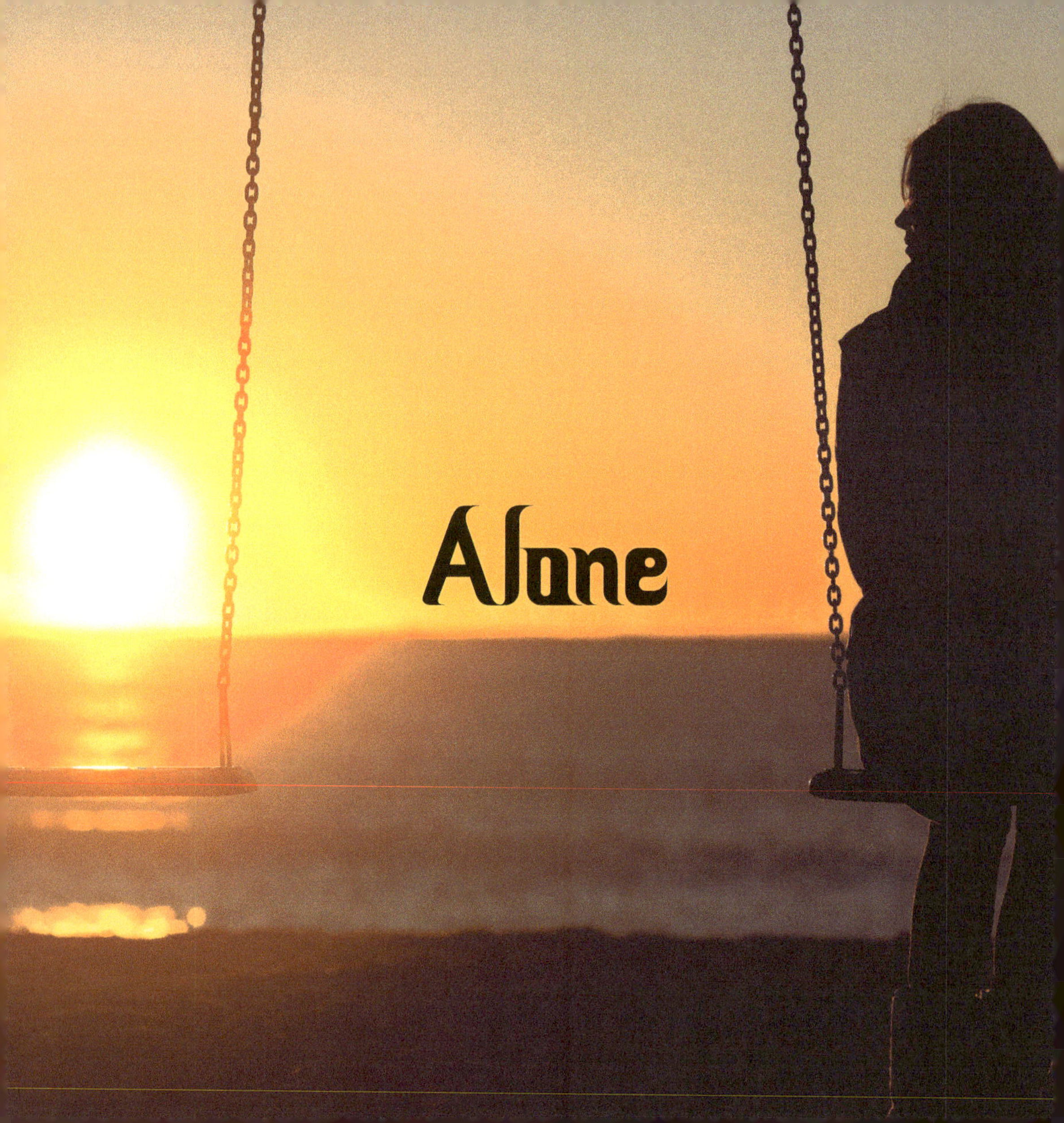
Alone

Who Am I

I told myself I was no one
And someone else agreed
I told myself no friends had I
And friends I did not need.
Someone inside said live alone
You really need no one
Don't give or take or share your love
Don't laugh or ever have fun.
Just hate and be like all you see
Don't understand the other guy
Just stay alone, all to yourself
And alone you'll surely die.

My days are lonely
And nights are too
I look and search
For only you
You promised me
Long, long ago
You would be here
My hand to hold
We've gotten lost
Along the way
I need your love
Both night and day.

As One

Remember when we started out
We laughed, had so much fun
We loved and shared so many things
We tried to be as one.
The Lord looked down and sent to us
His blessings from above
He gave us children and a home
To care for and to love.
He blessed us both with health and joy
And peace He did provide
We faced together the good and bad
In our hearts, love did abide.
We're growing old, time's running out
Let's laugh and have some fun
Let's grow together, not apart
Our hearts should be as one.

BEST OF THE BEST

BEST OF THE BEST

BEST OF THE BEST

BEST OF THE BEST

BEST OF THE BEST

BEST

OF THE

BEST

Be The Best

A writer must write
A painter must paint
And be what he can be.
A singer must sing
A dancer must dance
To live here joyfully.
To be the best at what you do
And following God's plan
Brings joy and peace while on this earth
Contentment for the man.

I loved you long before; you were a child upon this earth
I love you now, I loved you then, even before your birth.
While you were just a little form deep inside of me
I knew who you were before the eye could see.
You were so fair, so sweet and small, my heart with love
o'erflowed
Throughout the years you've grown more dear,
the depth you'll never know.
I thank the Lord and praise His name, he's been so kind
and true
Because he gave to me a child—because he sent me you.

When I was just a little one,
Each night my mother said—
"Call me if you need me"
As I got into bed.
If I had a bad dream or couldn't sleep for fear,
Sure enough, I'd call, and she would come—I knew that she
was near.
But as the years went by, and I was on my own
I needed no one, although I felt alone.
Then one day, I heard someone say that familiar line again
"Call me if you need me" Dear Lord, I need a friend.

Could you know my needs
Without words ever said
Could you care enough
To look inside my head
Could you take the time
To love me—only me
Could you help me be
All that I want to be?

When the night air's crisp
And the moons bright yellow
I long to cuddle
With my favorite fellow
Being all alone
Feeling warm and close
No telephones ring
We're cut off from most
All lovey and snuggly
Without care or worry
Just me and my fellow
Living life without hurry.

Don't Laugh

Don't laugh at me
I'm not a clown.
When you make fun
I'm upside down.
Are you so good
And me so bad?
You may not know
The life I've had.

Dreams

When I was young and in my teens,
I was so foolish and full of dreams
But as I aged and out-grew dreams,
I got so wise, or so it seemed
I thought I knew a lot more than the average woman or
average man
I tried to live like a grown-up, I put away foolish dreams
and plans
I soon found out dreams can be real, they somehow
express how we feel
So if you have a special dream to you, keep right on
dreaming it may come true.

Empty Nest

My nest now is empty
The children are grown
The house feels deserted
As I sit here alone.
The windows need cleaning
The shutter torn down
No longer doors slamming
No more cruising the town.
No more noses to wipe
No more rocking to sleep
The Boston sits empty
Its loving arms weep.
What happened to skinned knees
Mending hearts that were broken
I've replaced them with memories
More precious than token.
So I'll place all these memories
In my heart for today
And I'll find joy tomorrow
I will find a new way.

Get excited about your life
Be positive, have fun
You're here but such a short time
Very soon your life will be done.

Tears I see
My days are blue
My nighttime too
What will I do?
I was so true
He said to me
That he would be
Forever true
What will I do?

Home

Our old house is still standing
I see it almost every day
Although it's changed, I still see
It the way it used to be
The kitchen so warm and cozy
On the coldest winter's day
The bread all hot from the oven
It always tastes better that way
The soups in the pot
The tick of the clock
And father's at home at last
The supper may be simple
But the love is ample
To chase all the cold away.

How Long Lord

I wonder what went wrong
What turns I failed to make
Did I give away too much
Was love afraid to take?
My life has seemed so hard
This shame that's cast on me
I hid it oh so well
So no one else would see
What warped the thoughts and mind
The lines of trust tore down
Seems I go thru life's dark maze
My face wears a silly frown
How long Lord, just how long
Must I bear this agony
When will the sun shine thru
When will it shine for me?

I Count

I'm standing right here
Can't someone see?
I have a voice
Someone hear me!
I know I count
I do my best
I'm still right here
Can't someone see?
Then I listen, and I feel
Your presence in my soul
I know I've been redeemed
Cleansed and made whole.

I do not know the time of day
My Lord will call me home;
I cannot tell you where I'll be
Just where my steps may roam.
I only pray my heart will be
Ready on that day,
To hear His voice, to see His face,
I'll find a better way.

To do 'My Thing' is to live for you
And try to please you in all I do;
I get my 'High' when I feel you near
And your sweet voice inside I hear.

WHO AM I

I Know Now

In the rhythm of your world
I find such a peace and rest
In the beauty all around
I see my soul as blest
At last inside, I feel
Part of God's special plan
I know I am your child
I know now who I am

I love this day you've given me
The rain, the sun this life
I love it when you speak to me
Through good times or through strife
I love to feel you close inside
When I kneel down to pray
You take my cares, my sins,
My burdens all away.

YOU
are
important

I Matter

You know I matter
I'm important too.
I need you to hear
What I say to you.
I want to scream
Can't someone understand?
Won't someone care
Please take my hand?
Why close your ears
Close your heart off too?
I know I'm important
I should matter to you.

I know what I don't like, what makes me turn away
But sometimes I forget the things that make my day!
The little things the people do, those near to me who care
They help me in such tender ways, my work they help
me share.
If I forget to say I care, my love, I'll fail to show
Forgive me Lord make them aware, my thanks, You let
them know.

I'd like to know you

I'd like to know you
Know where you go
What fears you have
What things you know
What makes you sad
What makes you cry
Why that lonely look
Is in your eye
If we could be friends
And you would trust me
Maybe I could help
Maybe then I'd see.

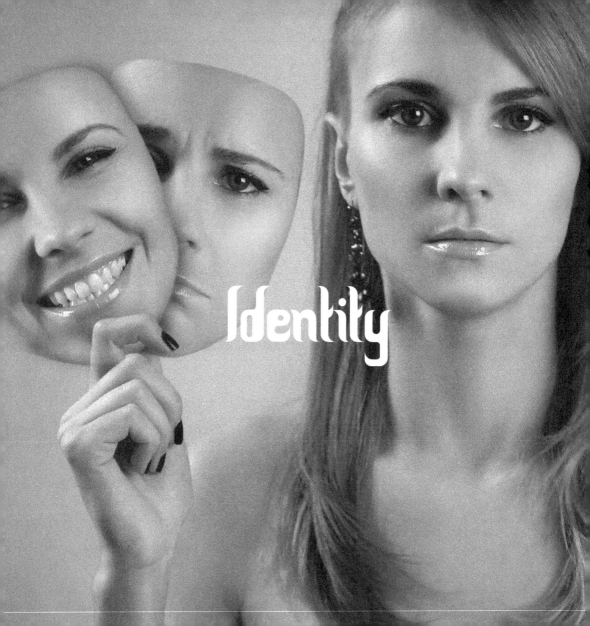

I feel like just a form, a small face in the crowd
A being without a name, a voice that's not too loud
If I could find a love to share my joys and fears
He'd hold me thru the night and wipe away my tears
But would I dare to dream, this dream I've had so long
He'd love as I am, He'd love me right or wrong
I would no longer be without identity
I'd share my dreams with him, he'd share my life with me.

If I can do some deed today, pleasing unto Thee
If I can show someone the way, this day, I've lived for Thee.
If I can touch some lonely heart, by something said or done
If I can help to ease the pain, the victory you have won.

If You
Knew

If you knew tomorrow, you would die
Would you cause another pain or make someone cry?
Or would you take some time with folks you hold dear
And try to lift them up and bring them hope and cheer.
Would you spend some time down on your knees in prayer
Today is almost gone, tomorrow will soon be here.

I'll Be
Brave

I tell myself I'll be okay
Not care if left behind
I'll live my life as always
Be brave, won't really mind.
I won't miss conversations
Or walks around the block
Won't miss the hugs and kisses
Picking up dirty socks
Won't miss just lying close to him
Sipping coffee late at night
Won't miss the loving after
A silly little fight
Won't miss long drives together
When he needs to unwind
I tell myself I'll be okay
Be brave—won't really mind.

In the winter of my life

In the winter of my life
I found what it means to live
I have time to reflect
And know what it means to give
In the spring when I was young
And I learned to use my wings
I thought happiness was bought
With money and pretty things
Then summer came to me
I was busy night and day
I had no time for you
I did not stop and pray

When I feel something deep inside that I know is
wrong or right,
I know, Dear Lord, that is you saying not to lose sight.
I get so sure and plunder in, sometimes without a prayer,
Just trusting my own self—and then I hit a snare.
But when I take the time and ask, for you right there to be,
I know you are inside and care, inside deep down in me.

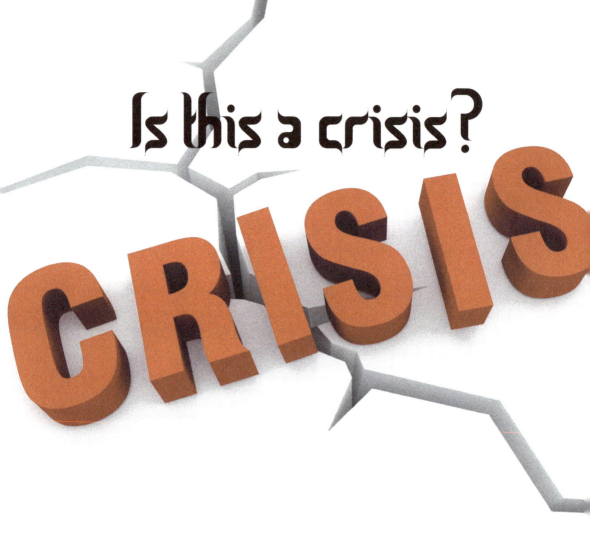

I can't understand
These things I feel
Are they make-believe
Or are they real?
My mind gets crazy
Then I cry a lot
I get real clammy
Then I get real hot
No one understands
No one seems to care
My feelings get hurt
Seems there's no one there
I just work all day
Can't sleep for this strife
Is this a major crisis
Or is it change of life?

It's Almost Like She's Here

It's almost like she's here
Sweet memories remain
Her perfume fills the air
The fragrance still the same
Her clothes so neatly hung
The shoes all in a row.
Her toothbrush in its place
The sweater worn and old.
Why did she go away?
The one I loved so dear
Her presence fills my heart
It's almost like she's here.

It's not me Lord who writes these words
But your sweet voice inside I've heard
I just put down what I hear you say
Your gentle voice I will gladly obey.

Who Am I

January feels like a Monday
Where do I go from here?
Is this a new beginning
Or the end of another year?
Springtime feels so far away
The days are dark and long
The robin just cannot be found
I do not hear his song
I now have time to do little things
And make some great big plans
To settle down and get in touch
And find out who I am

Don't let me be like that other guy
So angry, so greedy and so shy.
Please keep me humble, and obey your word
So your still small voice can be heard.

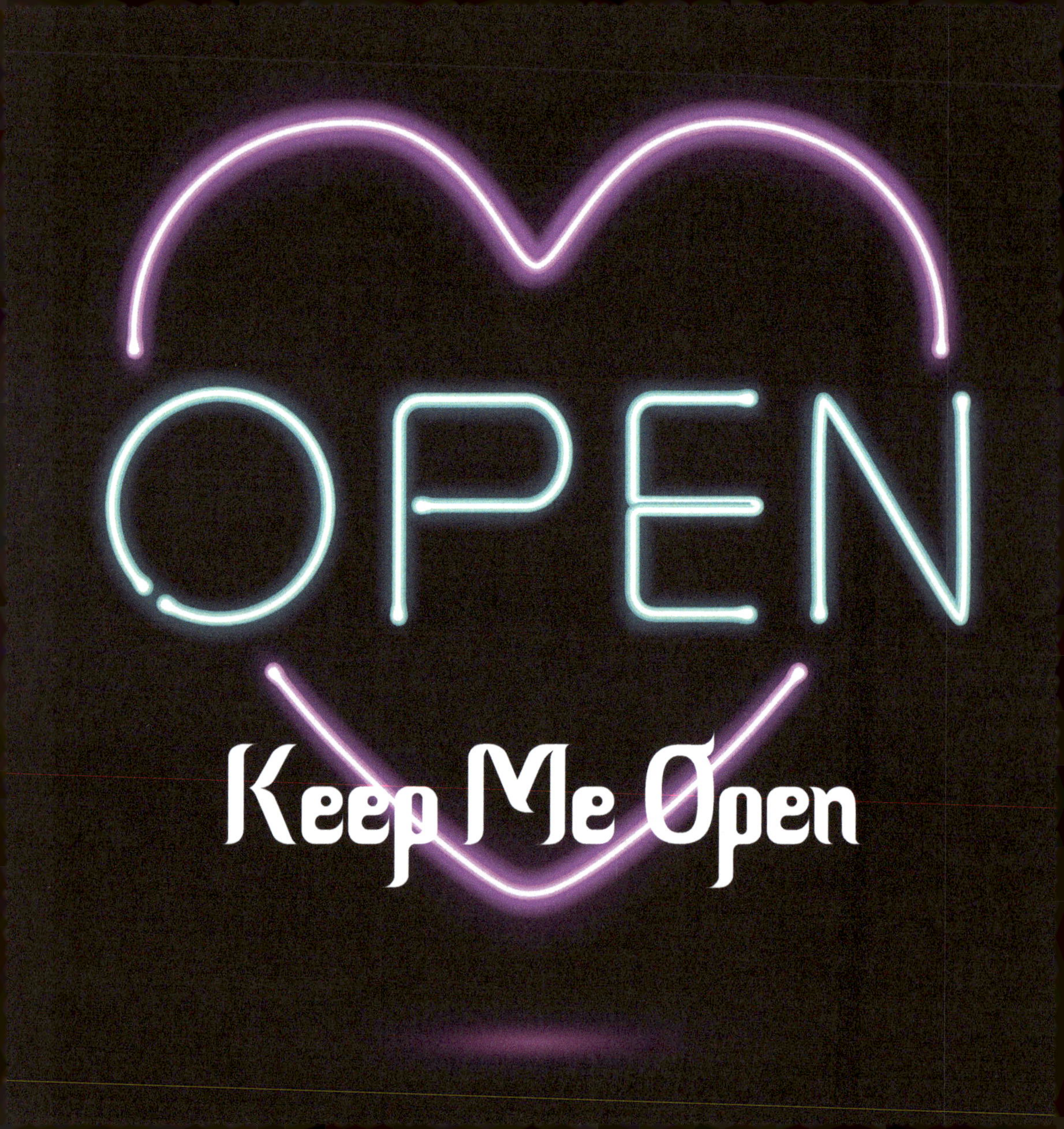
OPEN
Keep Me Open

The things inside I feel and know
With your love will flourish and grow;
When I am open to your love, your way
I can always hear, Lord, what you say.

I'd like to be your friend
I'll listen to your fears
I'll be there when you hurt
I'll help to dry your tears.
I'd like to help you thru
If only you'd let me in
I'll not betray your trust
I'd like to be your friend.

Who Am I

I caught myself a-whistlin'
Had a smile upon my face
I felt as if I was ten feet tall
Like a giant in that tiny space.

My eyes were wide and full of glee
Not a worry or complaint
I felt as I could do all things
Could be something that I ain't.

My step had a certain springy bounce
Like an energetic child
My voice was slightly out of range
Not its normal soft and mild.

You asked me what has taken place?
Someone complimented me today
They made me feel important
Listened to what I had to say.

Who Am I

I think I'll give this up
Not write these little rhymes
Not clutter up my brain
Nor take up all my time.
Nor tell someone nearby
How much I really care
Or let them know they're liked
And in my daily prayers
But then I stop and think
This is a part of me
The words come from my heart
For others to read and see
So I'll just keep right on
Taking up precious time
Writing little notes
And rhyming little rhymes.

How do I measure by those around
On life's small-scale am I up or down?
Do I dress and act just like I should
Would I be better if only I could?
Do I fit right in with any crowd
Or am I weak or do I act proud?
Do I help those people who are in despair
Or turn away and not really care?
Lord in my heart I know you see
Help me to measure up to Thee.

My Blindness

Why put my trust in men on earth
Instead of trusting Thee?
I know deep down inside Dear Lord
You never have failed me.
So when I fail to lean on you
It's just that I can't see.
The blindness, please remove
So I can live for Thee.

My
Dad

He did the very best he could, he loved his family
He was not always strong, his way we did not see
He was so good at all he did and worked hard every day
Perhaps it just was too much for him, too many bills
to pay!
He did not fit into a mold, no man was made the same
He gave me life, he was my dad, I proudly bear his name.

My Family

My family is just plain folks put here by God above

They do not have riches or fame but hearts so full of love

They may not dress real fancy—fine or live in luxury

But they possess the greatest gift this world will ever see

They all have love and tenderness they give to show
they care

I thank the Lord for each of them they're in my
every prayer.

My Gain

I may not always do what's right, I do not always smile;
I get so mired down, at times I cry awhile.
I do not always trust you, Lord, to take away the pain;
I often forget that all my loss is really all my gain.

Since I was just a little girl, my mother prayed for me,
She asked the Lord to take good care and from the
devil flee.
I always knew a hand was guiding me on my way along,
Showing me what was right, showing me what was wrong.
I know she's up in heaven with all the angel hosts,
Singing praises to the Father, the Son, and the Holy Ghost.

In December we're sometimes guilty
Of going in such a rush
We do not always show our love
Show how deep and just how much
We overlook the small little things
Ignore those people who care
Our days are hurry scurry
Little things don't stand a prayer
We say some things we should not say
At times don't say enough
The pace just overwhelms us
We act like ol' man Gruff
But when we finally settle down
And look at where we are
We give our time and share our love
With people near and far
So we make a pledge to start anew
And begin again next year
To love our neighbor and our God
While on this earth we're here

May I forget the past, the mistakes along the way
Help me to look ahead—to live tomorrow and today
Please guide my path, thy way make plain
I'll sing your praise forever and ever—I ask in Jesus name.

These words are my thoughts, what I feel in my heart
You may not believe all or even a small part
They were put in me by my God above
To point the way and show you his love.

My Wealth

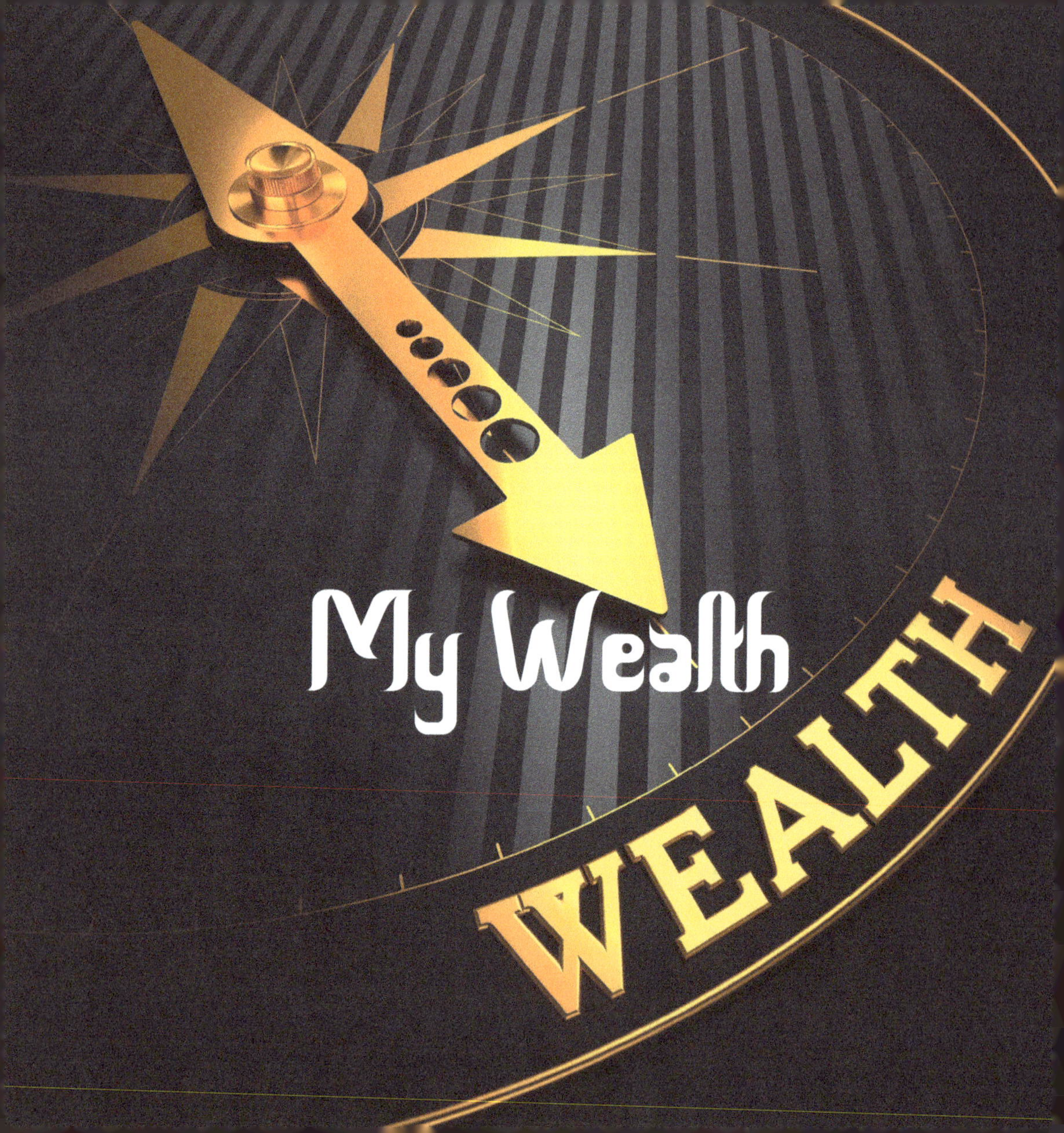

Some people have so many riches, they have power, beauty,
and fame;

They own big homes and speak so fine, have titles with
their names.

But I am just a plain ol' me, made by my God above;

My wealth is His forgiveness, His power, and His love.

My Work

We all are here a very short time
Our days are numbered, true.
I pray, Dear Lord, help me to find
The work you'd have me to do.

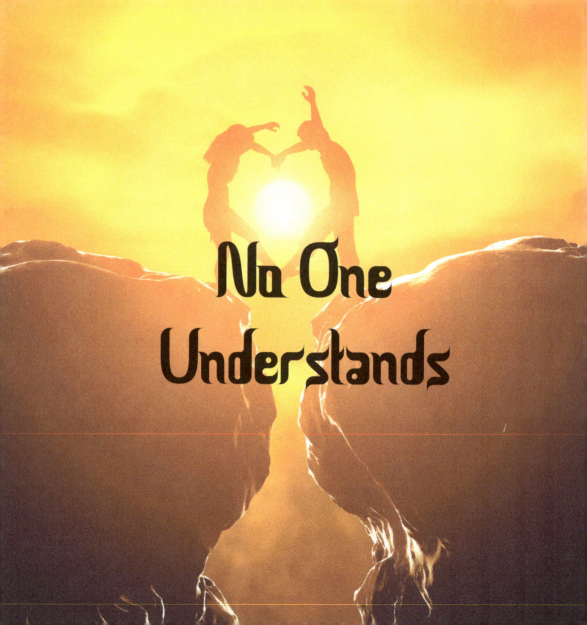

No one understands me
I wonder if they try?
My heart hurts deep inside me
Some days I sit and cry.
Then other times I am so strong
Like I need no one here;
I go around just like a clown
So full of hope and cheer.
Am I so wrong or did I do
Some tragic dread offense?
Why can't we love, is there still time
This does not make much sense.
I'd love to love you
So wild and free;
Let down defenses
And just be me.
I'd love to accept you
And you accept me;
I'd love to love you
And have you love me.

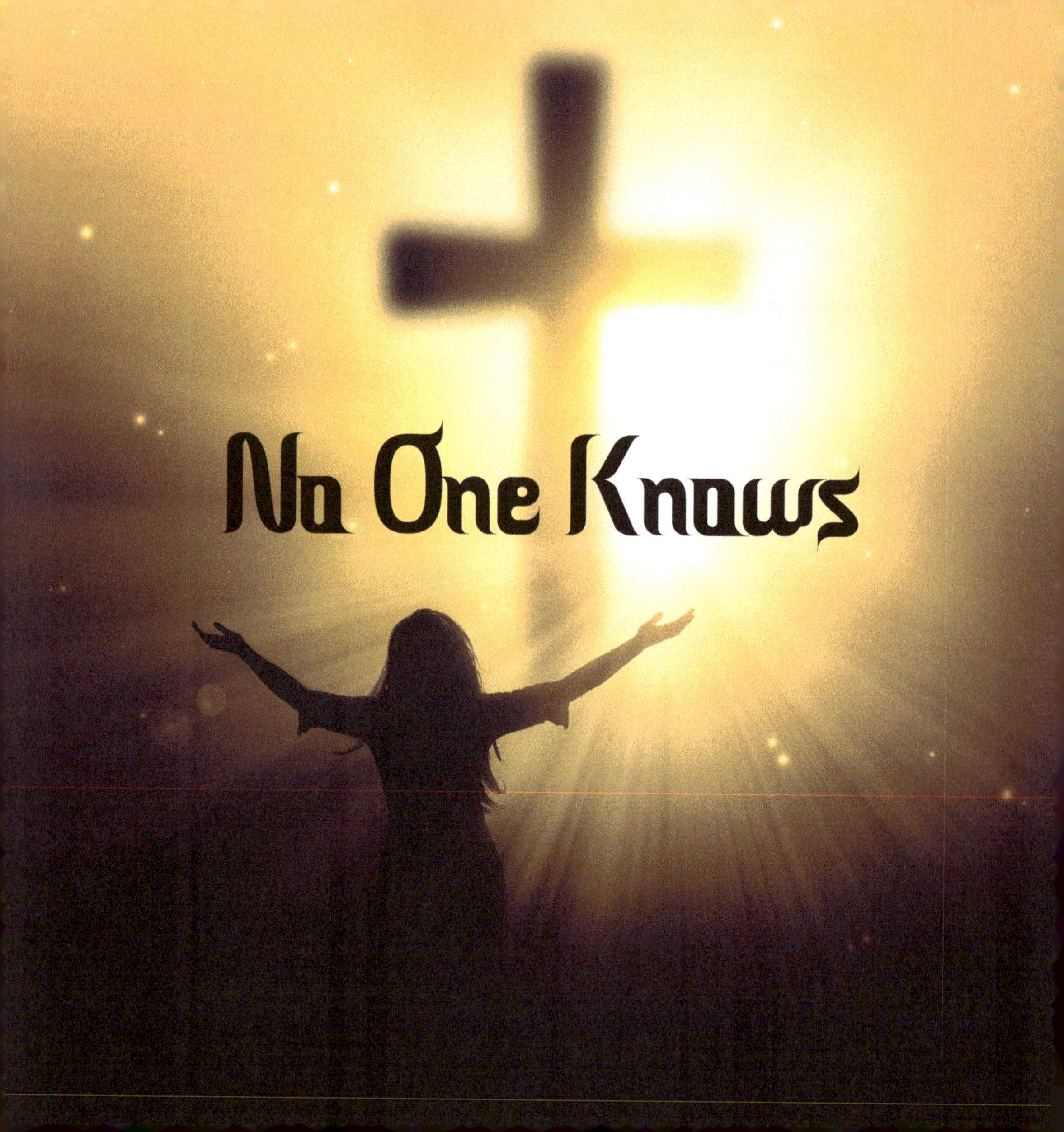
No One Knows

No one knows about those dreams
Or the pain my body felt
No one saw my agony
My hand here no one held
They could not feel the awful load
From all my sin and shame
You bore it all and pardoned me
And loved me all the same.

Numb or
Motionless

Sad eyes know not teardrops
While the lonely heart cries
The soul longs for laughter
Each day spirits die
Just an endless last journey
Without feeling or pain
Not feeling the sunshine
Not feeling the rain
Just motionless motions
Painless pain without cure
Their journey continues
How long to endure?

Who Am I

I love old barns that smell of hay
They remind me of a lazier day.
When times were slow and lots of fun
Especially when the work was done.
We'd wade in streams that overflowed
And have ballgames out in the road.
We'd play with dolls and braid our hair
Our folks were there we knew they cared.
We'd go to church til noon on Sunday
We'd sing the songs, believe what they'd say.
Then after the work and play was through,
Lord, I'd go to the barn and talk to you.

Old Woman

Get moving old bones
What need to complain?
You've got to keep moving
In the sun and the rain.

Get to thinking old brain
Can't you figure things out?
You'll get left behind
Without a doubt.

Old eyes can't you see
What you need to see?
You're not looking clearly
Taking care of me.

Now blood you start
flowing
Flowing through real swift;
We depend on you
For that special lift.

Now spirit get with it
Cause we need a boost;
Who else can we count on
Who else can we trust?

Old woman keep going
Do your very best;
The Lord will help you
And your days He'll bless.

Who Am I

Out on the porch
In the back of our home
I feel pure contentment
It's a place all my own.

A friend will stop by
For a visit—a chat
Not much going on there
I'm real happy 'bout that.

It's not furnished real fancy
Nor furnished real fine
It's a lifetime of treasures
A collection in time.

I spend a lot of my days
In the back of my home
No need to go elsewhere
No longer needing to roam.

I'm surrounded by nature
I can hear the birds sing
As I watch the sun rise
What a marvelous thing.

I'm just a plain ol' fashioned girl and sometimes
not too smart;

But, Lord, you know the love I feel comes right
straight from the heart.

At times I am confused, slow down and lose my way,

And other days I just stand back not knowing what to say.

If you'd forgive me one more time and help me
find your plan,

Just help this ol' fashioned girl; I'm ready
for your command!

The richest lady, that's what I am,
I have no need to wear a crown.
To some, I may not have too much—
As far as jewels, cars and such.
But I have Jesus Christ inside me
And so I'm very rich you see.

You are the one man whom I love,
How much you'll never know.
We've had our bad times also good,
But that's the way we grow.
You've been there when I needed you,
You've always been my friend.
I pray the Lord, stay by my side
Until our life shall end.

Stay With Me

I'll always love you
Come what may
Please stay with me
We'll find a way
I'll let you be
Who you want to be
I'll always love you
Could you love me?

Why are we strangers still
After all these many years?
Why do we run away
Keep hiding unwept tears?
Am I the one to blame
Can't I just be your friend?
Why are we strangers still
When will the silence end?

I wish I could go inside of you
To find what makes you happy and blue.
I cannot tell just by your sighs
Or that lonely look deep in your eyes.
If you can't say the word real clear
I cannot guess at words I don't hear.

Sharing tender moments without a word
Hearing thoughts only our hearts have heard
Being in tune and keeping in touch
Sharing those moments and loving so much.

The Conductor

I met an ol' conductor
Whose life was all about trains
He didn't have great wealth or
fortune
Never reached great heights of
fame.

He was a wise old gentleman
Wise in the ways of life
He knew what kept us all on track
Keeps our lives here free from
strife.

He'd talk about the long
smooth track
And the bed under which it laid
It was not wrought of steel or iron
But of rock and stone was made.

How our lives are sometimes
like that track
Not smooth along the way
We get confused and get
sidetracked
Don't know what to do or say.

At last, we know we have to stop
To get refueled and then
We take a break then look
around
Then start right up again.

So like the ol' conductor
We learn as we travel on
To stay on track and do our best
Til the prize someday we've won.

The
Gift

Who Am I

Perhaps a vase
An expansive treat
Or an item large
Something to eat
Or maybe something
Purchased long ago
Or someone so dear
Someone I know
Whatever the gift
Whatever the price
The message comes thru
About love and life
I give so freely
And wish sincere
That peace will come
To you this year.

The Good Ol' Days

Whenever I think of the good ol' days
I remember long walks and how we'd play
We knew each person who lived on our street
We'd smile and talk each time we'd meet,
We always had time our love to show
We'd say it out loud so others would know,
And when a friend needed someone near
We'd bake a pie and spread good cheer.
We knew just who our God was then
In the good ol' days, He was our friend.

Who Am I

I sit and wonder
My mind a whirl
My vision unclear
My soul a furl
What does it mean
This life and journey
What prize to win
What really matters
Do I live to please
Just me—only me
Or strive to help
Someone in need
This road is long
And travelers are we
Someday we'll rest
Reach our destiny
So I'll toil today
Cause my days are few
And I'll let love flow
From me to you.

The Place

Who Am I

Remember when you were a dream
Hid neath your mother's breast
She nourished you and gave you love
You felt so warm and blest.
That place was safe, secure and warm
You wanted to stay and stay
The world was big, you were so small
Could you survive one day?
But loving arms took care of you
And you grew to love this place
The Lord took care and nourished you
With His tender love and grace.
This land is safe, you feel so secure
You want to stay and stay
But God has promised a better life
A cloudless, glorious day.
He'll take you there thru death's golden door
That leads to Heaven above
If you believe in His precious Son,
His pardon and His love.

The Puzzle

Are you going around in circles, looking for a clue?

Trying to find some answers, of what you are to do?

The more you search and look around the more you
are confused;

Try looking up to God, he'll solve the puzzle for you.

The Secret

Secret

Who Am I

When I was young, I'd sit and dream
I'd play with dolls and want nice things
I'd want to be in another place
Looking thru eyes from another face
I thought if I possessed great wealth and fame
All men on earth would know my name
If beauty men saw when they looked at me
Then beauty would mean everything to me
But soon I learned that money and fame
Don't mean a thing in life's big game
The secret of life at last I see
As real happiness lies deep inside me.

This country where I work and live
Has opportunities to give,
Freedoms we can all enjoy
Jobs to which we find employ,
We can worship when and where we please
There's cities and places for us to see,
We can spend our money without a care
Or hoard it all or we can share,
We can raise our children as we see fit
Or leave this place if we tire of it,
Our God has blessed us can't you see?
He's been so good to you and me!

The sky is blue, and the sun is high
My soul longs to rejoice and magnify
Your glorious name and sing your praise
You've been with me thru all the days
You've watched and kept me thru the night
And Lord you know we've had such a fight
Now show me what you'd have me to do
This day is yours, help me get through

This Game of Life

Who Am I

I've sat and watched you progress—
And observed you as you star
I know with your great talent—
Someday you will go far.
I'd like to tell you one thing—
About this game, we play
Just thank the Lord for all things
And watch each word you say.
I think you're someone special
And I'm proud that I know you.
Remember, makes no difference where you go
To you, you must be true.

Would you be there for me, whenever I need a friend?
To cherish and share my joy, until our days shall end.
To understand, or try, whenever I'm angry and cross
To have respect and not grow weary or try to be my boss,
To love and care when beauty no longer you see.
To be my friend forever, to be right there for me.

Sometimes I'd like to go way back

And be a child for a day

To once again relive good times and

Hear what others say

To be carefree and dream my dreams to laugh and run
and play

To just go back and be a child and

Be loved again that way

To Just Believe

Believe

I need to feel your presence, every minute, every day
I long to know your love, no matter what others say
To feel secure and not give up when storms toss me about
To just believe and keep on going and never ever doubt.

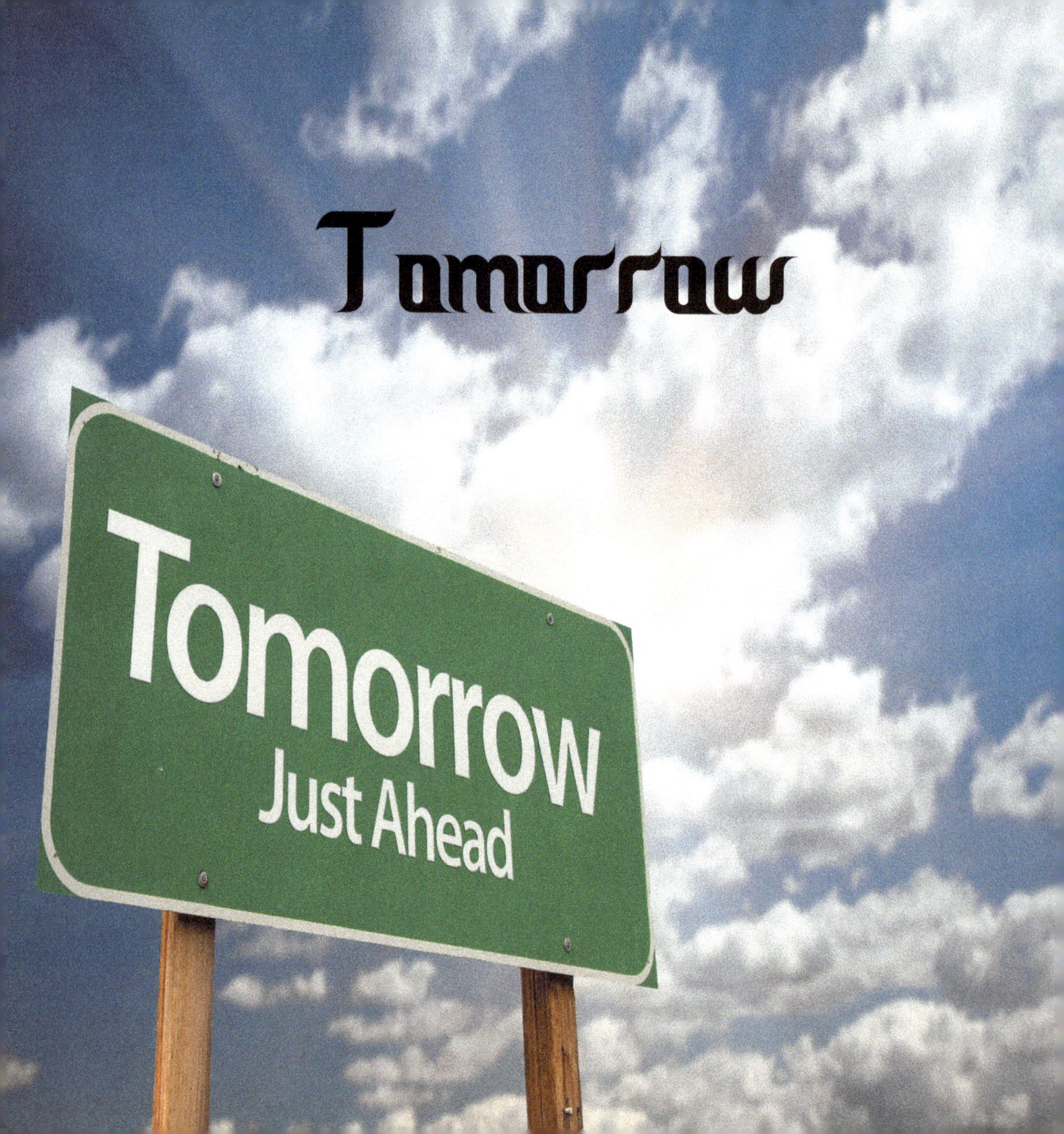
Tomorrow
Tomorrow
Just Ahead

Who Am I

What lies ahead tomorrow
Do you really want to know
You may have pain and sorrow
Or your cup may overflow.

There may be fields of flowers
Or dreary nights and days
Your path could be so rugged
Or smooth along the way.

You might just have to travel
Alone—but for a while
And look and pray to God
To return that once used smile.

So be content to rest in Him
Continue to love and grow
What lies ahead tomorrow
That's not for us to know.

Too
Much?

Do I expect too much from him?
Does he give all he can?
If he gave more, I'd worship him
But Lord, he's just a man

Who Am I

I will not pass this way again
Or tarry here too long
I'm going to another place
A land where I belong
With God our Father and the saints
I'll live eternally
All those I've loved for oh so long
Again someday I'll see
You will not look upon my face
Or feel my touch again
Cause very soon I'm going to
A grand and glorious land.

Walk With Me

Walk With Me
Walk where I walk
Maybe then you'll see
Who I am, What makes me, me.

We are a part of a sinful world
But God is in control
We see some people in misery
But as Christians stand up—be bold.

The evil and injustice we see
'round each and every turn
For peace and understanding
Our hearts forever yearn.

His power was proven upon the cross
The final victory won
When Christ shed His blood for you and me
The Messiah, God's chosen son.

God's people will forever endure
We must watch the way we live
To keep a vigil both night and day
An' take care of what He gives.

So do not be complacent
As together we watch and pray
Take hold of the truth—The Word of God
To heaven, it points the way.

Who Am I

When I'm in front of people
I always feel real faint
I may look oh so strong and sure
But that's one thing I ain't
I feel my legs get wobbly
All rubbery like a tire
It may only take a minute
But it feels more like an hour
My palms and toes get sweaty
I think they may just drip
My mind goes blank, and I fumble
Like I'm in a dreary pit
My voice gets weak and shaky

Then I feel my panty-hose run
I can't believe I'm doing this!
Lord, is this what you call fun?
My tongue gets dry and sticky
I swallow—then drink a lot
I get real clammy then 'fore too long
I seem to get real hot
Now you may say its change of life
And that could be so true
But now you know what it takes for me
To bring this welcome to you.

What Is A Woman?

Who Am I

For some time I've wondered, what should a woman be
Always quiet and gentle or going around noisily
Doing her thing without a thought or a care
Or knowing her place and staying right there
Loving her man and staying with him
Helping him stand thru thick or thru thin
Always a listener to hear each heartache
A door always open, a haven to make
She'll open her heart and pour out her love
And ask the Dear Lord for help from above.

ff

What's A Man
Supposed to Be?

Who Am I

Is a Man supposed to shed a tear?
And is it okay to have some fear?
Do men ever need a kind word said?
Or is there something they really dread?
Men always look so brave and sure
As if a storm they could endure
Lord surely men have their needs too
Just help me love my man so true.

Spring BREAK

When I need a Spring Training Break

Who Am I

My mind is in an awful state
It's like I'm in a fog
My legs feel like a dead night
Like a great big dreary log.

My arms hang loose—thy tingle
And then they get real cold
It can't be that I'm a senior
Or that I'm getting old.

If I could only get away
To get a different view
It sure would make me feel just great
And chase away these blues.

So fly down—or bus me there
Just get me there any way
I certainly would love it
And it sure would make my day.

When Youth Has Gone

When sunlight I can't see
And the days go whizzing by
Sweet memories fill my mind
I will not sit and cry
When youth has gone
And it seems like just a dream
I'll thank God above
I've done it all it seems.

Who Am I

It seems you've gone away
Although I touch your hand
You do not hear my words
Your heart doesn't understand
You look just like a mime
The motions you go thru
How can I touch your heart
How can I get to you?

Where Do You Go?

Where do you go for your quiet time
When you're alone with God?
It could be in your own room
Or along some road you trod.
Its where you can ask for help
And thank Him for his care;
To talk with Him in private
And spend some time in prayer.

Who am I, I asked myself
I do not always know
Somedays I try to be another girl
Someone in fancy clothes.
I curl my hair all up
Put on my paint and then
I paste a smile upon my lips
Pretend I'm all-a-grin.
The whole world sees me just like this
All nice and pretty—secure.
But Lord, you see the inward parts
The heart and mind impure.
Thank you, Lord, for sending your dear Son
He cleansed and made me whole
I am your child, You're my God
That's all I need to know.

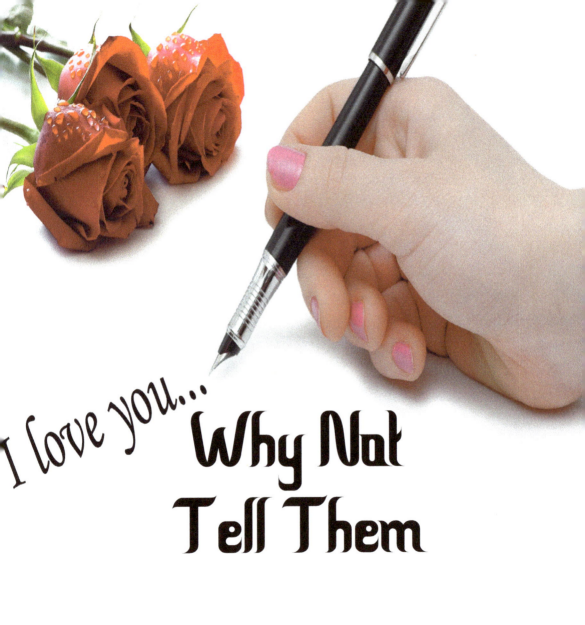

I love you... **Why Not Tell Them**

When you love someone so dear,
Why not tell them while they are here?
So soon our days will pass away
There'll be no time our love to say
We all need love, to give and share
To hear the words, 'I love you, I care'

Why can't I reach you,
What blocks my view?
Can't love keep flowing
From me to you?
My vision's lost
With words unsaid
Why can't I reach you—
Where has love fled?

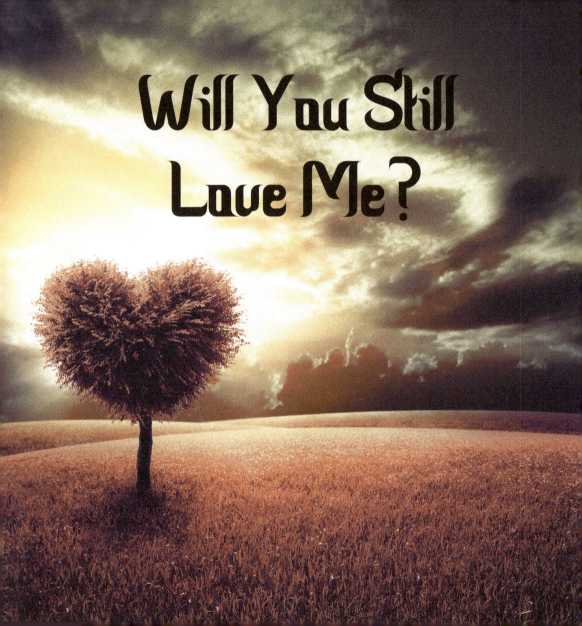

When I need a friend
Will you hold my hand?
When I feel lost and alone
Will you smile and say "I'm here."
When I act silly and forget who I am
Will you not forget me?
When I'm old, and beauty no longer you see
Will you still love me?

With You on
My Side

Perhaps I've never told you how much mean to me
I take for granted that you know, somehow that you can see
Without you here beside me, I'm nothing but a form
I'd go around so lifeless, soon I'd feel old and worn
But with you on my side, your commitment and love for me
I know I can do anything and be who I want to be

A woman's work is never done, we hear this every day
There's cooking, cleaning and yard work and also bills to pay
You bathe the children, feed the cat and iron pants and shirts
You hear the woes and dry the tears and bandage all the hurts
You pray Dear Jesus help me do my work as best I can
I'm just a woman, Lord, help me thru these pots and pans.

Who Am I

I reach out to touch your hand
I need you there to understand
Please take the time and hear me say
What's on my heart and mind today
Am I guilty of some crime
I need a friend—I need your time.

You're on my heart, you're on my mind
I long to know that you're just fine,
You know that you can count on me
When your clouds turn to gray.
If I can only say a word or offer a little prayer
I'd like to make your days much better
So I guess that's why I wrote this letter.

I know we're not the closest friends
But I still pray for you.
I pray the Lord to protect
And always care for you.
May he keep you in the shadow of his wing
And when dark clouds are overhead—his praises may we sing.

I will listen to your problems,
I will hold your hand each day,
I'll cry whenever you are hurt
I'll help to point the way;
I'll read to you God's Holy Word
And sing Amazing Grace,
But when the Lord speaks to your heart
I can't stand in your place.

CPSIA information can be obtained
at www.ICGtesting.com
Printed in the USA
LVHW070013060519
R14762200001B/R147622PG616485LVX1B/1/P